Outside and Inside MUMMIES

Sandra Markle

WALKER & COMPANY ● NEW YORK

This is a mummy, the preserved body of a person who lived long ago. Unlike a skeleton, a mummy still has skin and sometimes muscles and internal organs. Some mummies, like those of the ancient Egyptian pharaohs, were made by people. Others, like this mummy, were formed by nature.

Doesn't the mummy look mysterious? Imagine if it was possible to find out what this person was like alive: what she ate, how old she was, where she came from, and how she died. In this book, you'll find out how technology and new scientific methods are helping researchers solve those mysteries about people who lived a long time ago—and much more.

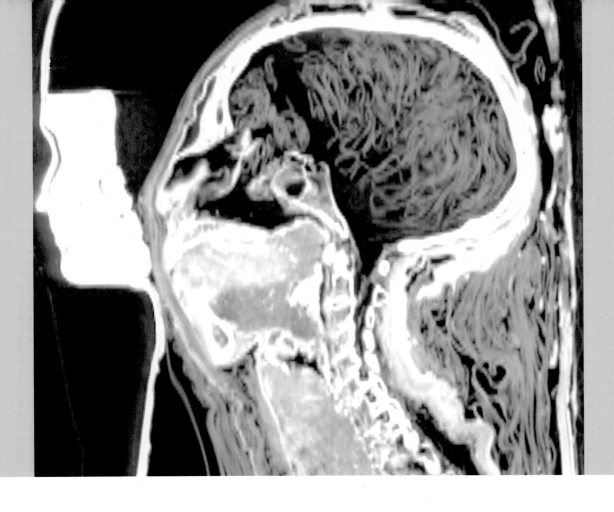

This is the head of a mummified ancient Egyptian man named Paankhenamun. People know his name because it's written on his coffin in hieroglyphics, the ancient Egyptian language. This image was produced when high-energy light rays called X-rays shot through the coffin and mummy and struck a special kind of photographic film. While photos show the outside of a body, X-rays reveal the hard bones and teeth that are inside.

Before the X-ray process was developed in the 1800s, the only way to see a mummy inside its coffin and wrappings was to open the case and unwrap it. To see the bones and internal organs, the body had to be cut open, and that spoiled it for any future investigation.

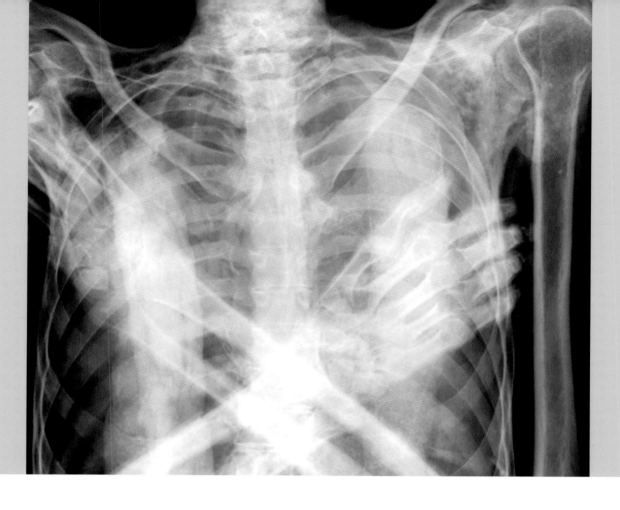

X-raying this mummy, above, provided some important clues. One clue, the position of his arms, revealed that he had probably been a pharaoh. In ancient Egypt, only pharaohs were buried with their arms crossed over their chests. And because the X-ray also revealed a certain amount of osteoarthritis (the wearing down of bones at the joints), it helped researchers determine that the person had been around forty-five years old when he died. These two valuable clues helped researchers decide the mummy was likely that of Pharaoh Ramses I.

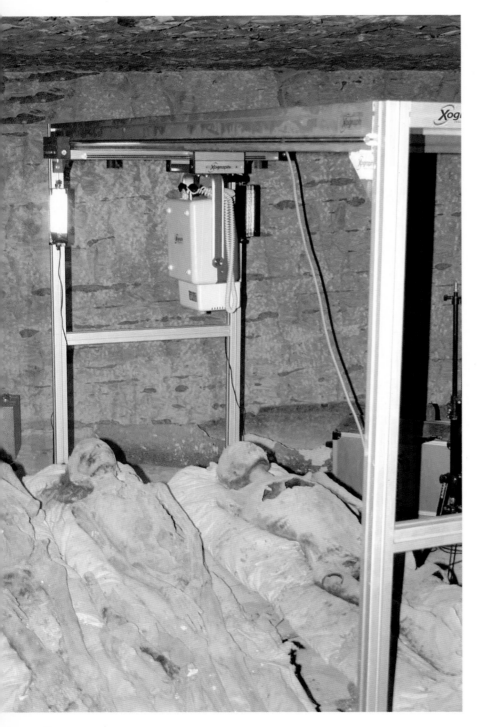

Most X-ray machines plug into a wall outlet in a clean environment near a photographic darkroom that's used to develop the special film. But in 2003, a state-of-the-art X-ray machine—the Canon CXD1-31 Portable Direct Digital X-ray—made it possible for researchers to investigate mummies deep inside a pyramid in Egypt. An electric generator supplied the power for the X-ray machine, a computer, and portable lights. Inside the pyramid, it was so hot that researchers were sweating heavily, and it was so dusty the computer screen had to be frequently wiped clean. Still, the Canon CXD1-31 worked perfectly.

As soon as this new X-ray machine was switched on and aimed at one mummy's head, X-rays passed through the body and struck the digital X-ray detector panel placed underneath. This sent signals to the computer, and, in just three seconds, an X-ray image of the mummy's skull appeared on the computer's screen. Because the results could be viewed almost instantly instead of waiting for film to be developed, the researchers were able to make adjustments that gave them the best possible view.

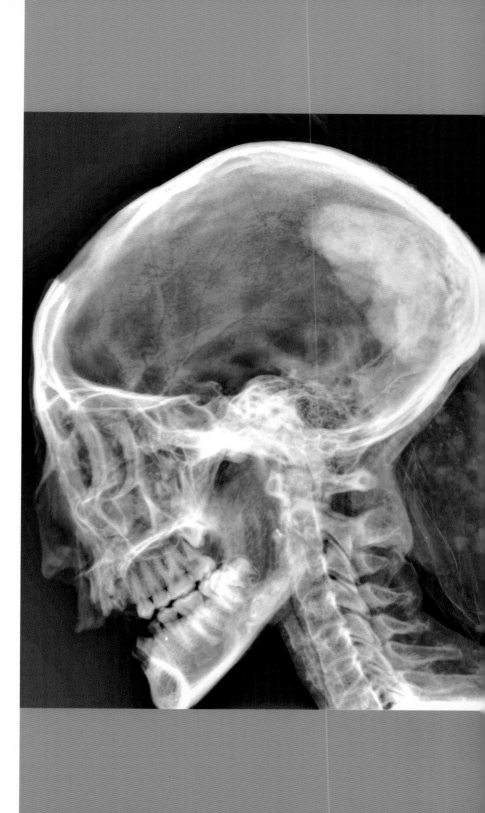

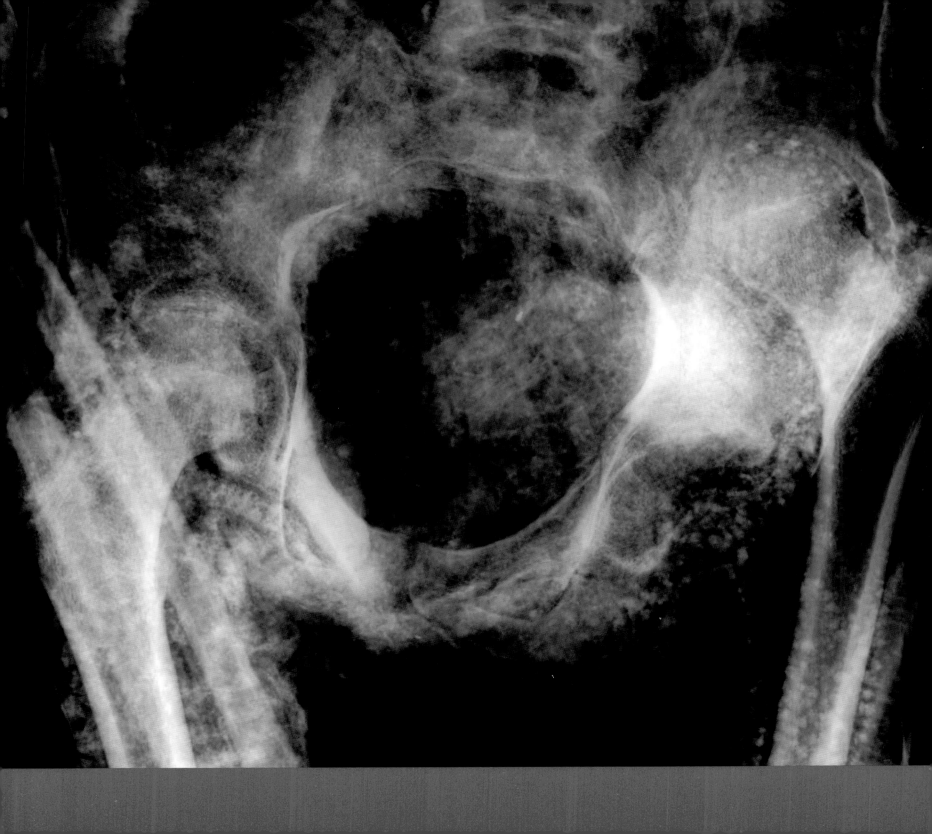

Take a close look at this mummy's hips to see an important clue researchers discovered while X-raying the mummies in the tomb. The end of one of the leg bones appears higher on the hip than the other. One of the mummy's legs must, at some time, have become dislocated so that it no longer fit properly into its socket. Because this injury would have made one leg shorter than the other, researchers learned that this person had almost certainly been unable to walk normally.

From the hip X-ray, researchers could also tell that this mummy was a male. Males have a narrower pelvic or hip structure than females. X-raying the hips of all three mummies in the tomb revealed that the other two mummies were females. This was an important clue for the researchers who suspected the three mummies to be Queen Nefertiti; Queen Tiy, grandmother of Tutankhamen—one of the world's most well-known mummies; and Tiy's eldest son, Tuthmosis.

Take a peek inside Pharaoh Ramses I's chest to see the ribs, the remains of the lungs, and linen-wrapped rolls of mummified organs. While the X-ray image on page 5 showed only the mummy's bones, this image also shows softer structures. It was made with the help of a special kind of X-ray machine called a spiral computerized axial tomography scanner, also called a spiral CT scanner. Now, read on to find out how this machine works and how it makes it possible to see body parts other than bones.

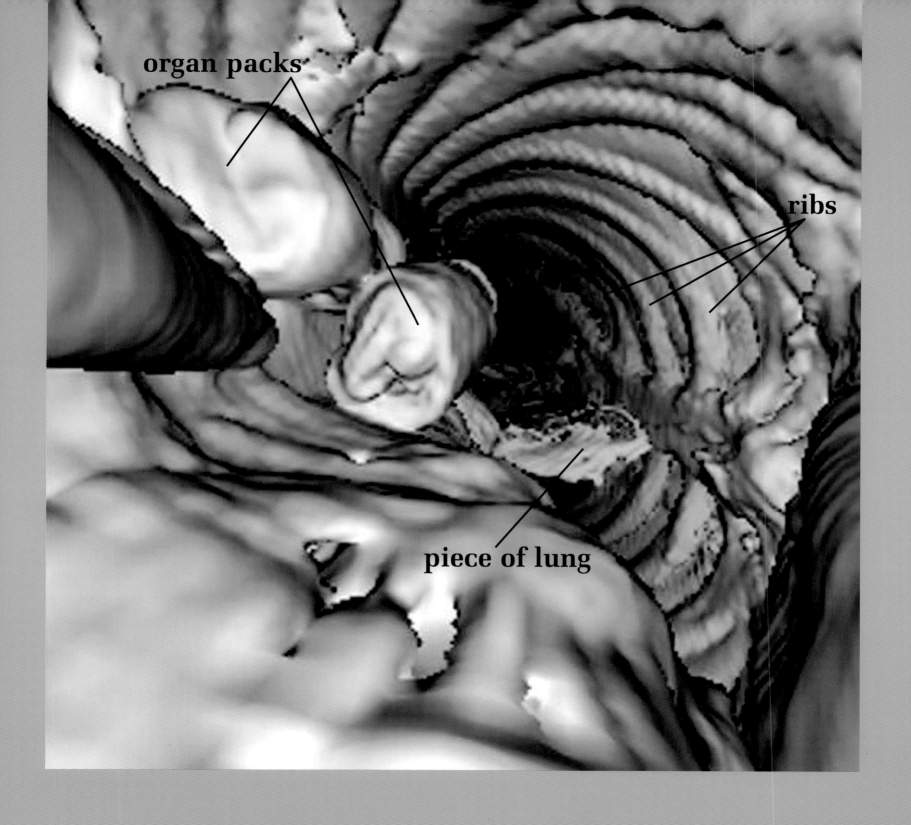

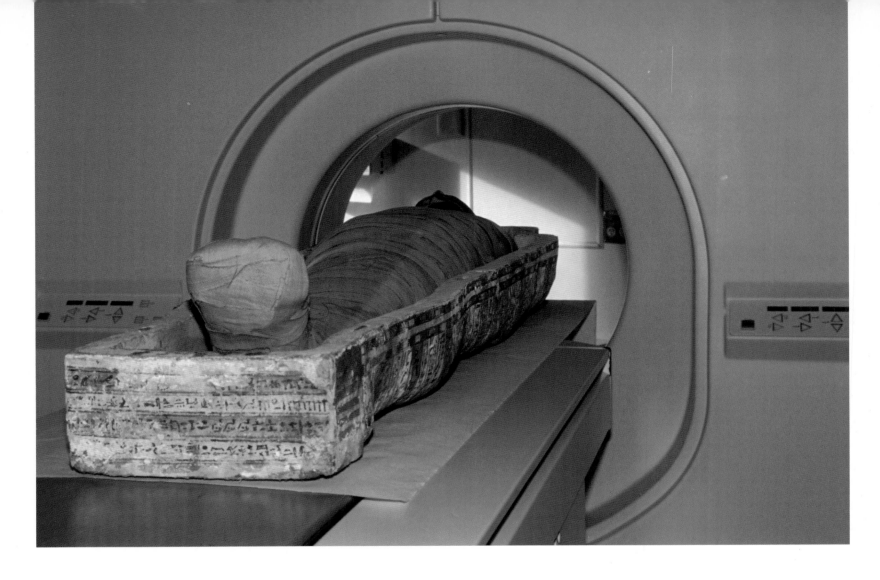

Here you can see the CT scanner. It's made up of an X-ray generating tube that continuously orbits the table as the mummy slides through the tunnel. Rather than being recorded on film, the images are recorded digitally by a computer. And the computer can be programmed to display images that show materials of different densities. So while an X-ray only shows parts made of solid material, like bones, a CT scan shows bones plus less dense parts, such as the body's internal organs.

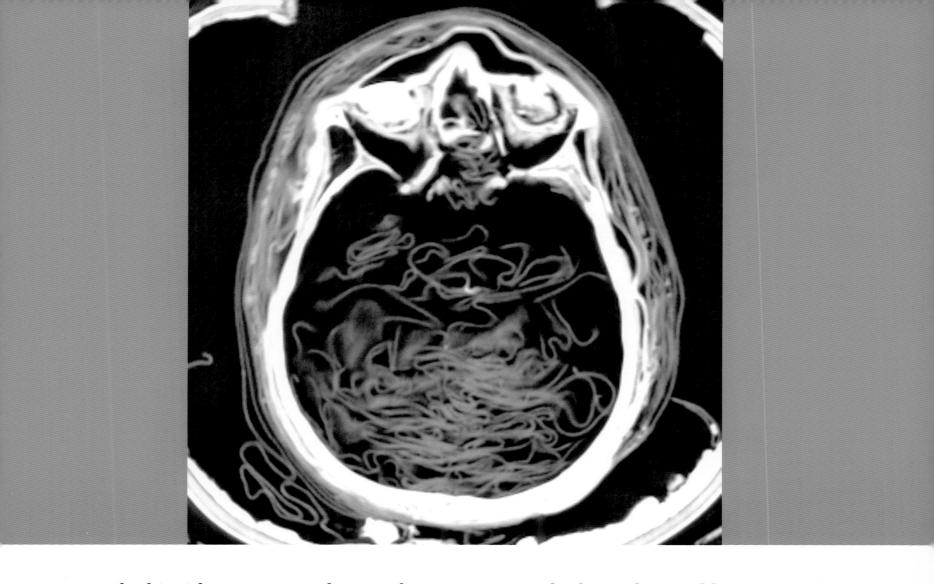

You peeked inside Ramses I's chest with an X-ray. Now look inside Paankhenamun's head with a CT scan. The squiggly gray lines are inside the skull where the brain should be, but they're just strips of cloth. In ancient Egypt, people thought all the brain did was produce the snot that drips out of noses. So oftentimes when a person was mummified, the soft brain tissue was removed. This was done, bit-by-bit, with a long, hooked needle inserted through the nose. Then strips of cloth were stuffed up the nose into the empty cavity.

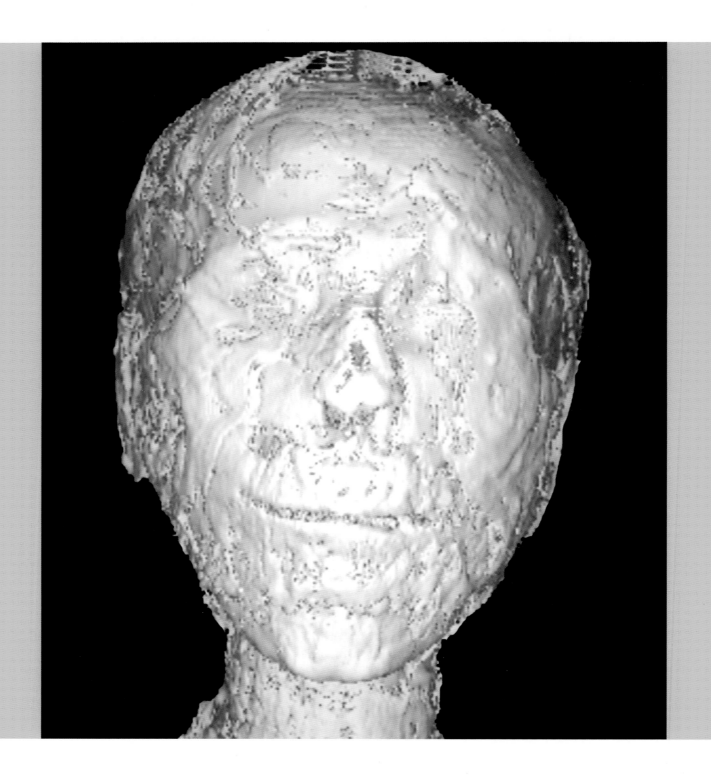

Now take a look at Paankhenamun's face. This picture was taken without unwrapping the mummy or even taking it out of its coffin. It was possible to reveal this view of Paankhenamun because the computer could be instructed to show an image made up of only material that was a specific density. To produce this image, the researchers first had to determine what density represented the mummy's skin. Then the computer had to be instructed to produce an image showing only materials of that density. The result is a peek at what Paankhenamun's face looks like under its cloth wrappings.

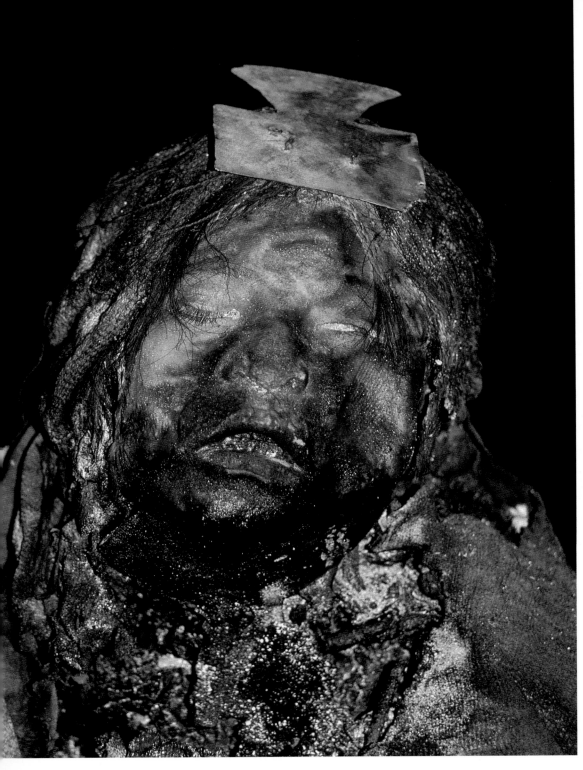

Other researchers used a different kind of technology to study the teeth of about sixty different mummies. These were mummies representing two groups of people living in South America: one living in the mountains and one living along the southern coast.

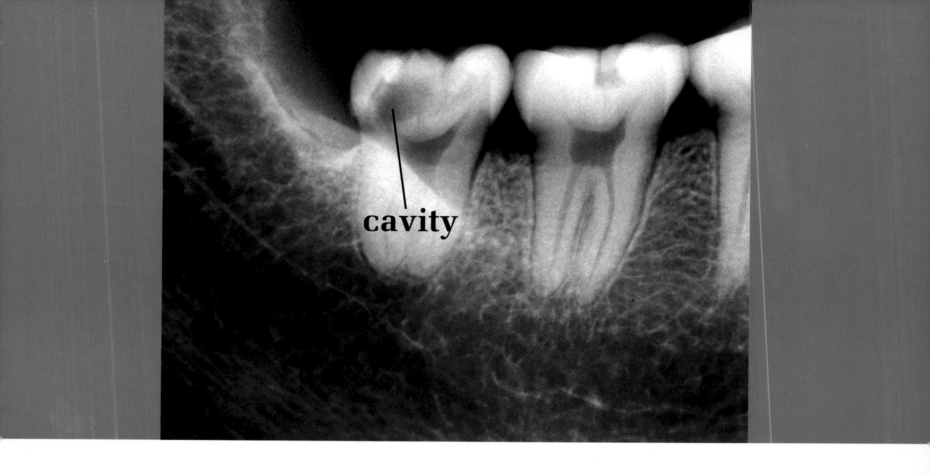

cavity

First, they blasted each mummy's teeth with an ion-beam accelerator. This device shot hydrogen atoms at the teeth and analyzed the particles released from the enamel, the hard material coating the tooth. The goal was to find out how much of a chemical called fluoride was stored in the enamel. They discovered that the teeth of the mountain mummies contained a lot whereas the teeth of the coastal mummies contained only a little. Then just the way dentists check today, researchers X-rayed the mummy's teeth, looking for cavities. They discovered that the people with a high level of fluoride had fewer cavities. Today, fluoride is added to water and toothpaste to help prevent cavities. Studying the mummies' teeth proved this chemical has a long history of preventing tooth decay.

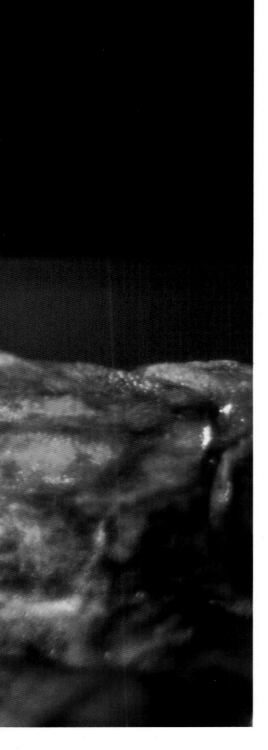

Imagine hiking in the Austrian Alps and discovering this mummified body! That's what happened in 1991 when a man and his wife discovered the Iceman, nicknamed Oetzi after the mountains where he was discovered. The couple notified the police, who at first thought this must be the remains of either a lost hiker or a murder victim whose body was dumped in the mountains. They had no idea how long the body had been there until they started digging it out of the ice that still held it trapped. Then they discovered an ancient-looking ax with a copper blade and other ancient-looking gear. They realized that this must be a very old mummified body.

So as soon as the body was removed from the ice, researchers started examining the Iceman. At first, because they discovered the pollen of autumn-blooming plants in the ice around Oetzi, researchers believed the Iceman was a shepherd who probably died in a fall snowstorm. When X-rays and CT scans revealed broken ribs, researchers guessed Oetzi might have fallen and then died. Some thought he might have fought with someone, then escaped into the mountains where, too weak to go on, he died. Later, however, with the help of new tools, researchers were able to discover new clues that changed their view of what had happened to Oetzi.

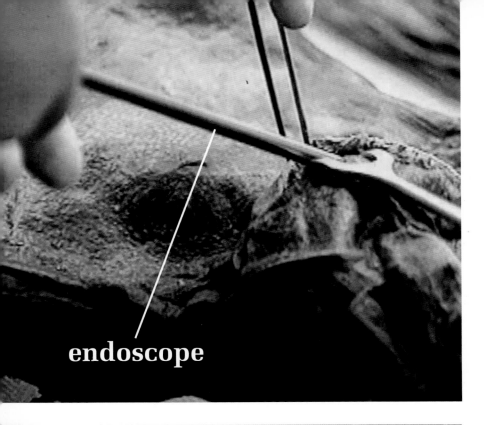

endoscope

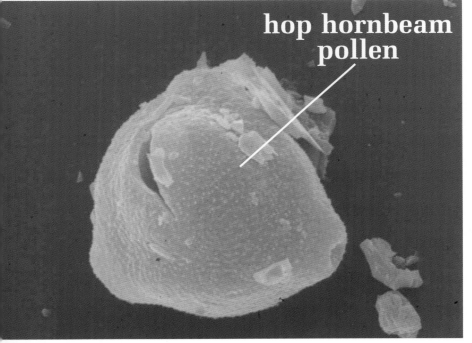

hop hornbeam pollen

One tool was this tiny camera on a flexible cable, called an endoscope, which was inserted into Oetzi's body. Connected to a computer, the endoscope let researchers see the Iceman's internal organs. Then they used a small tool attached to the cable to snip off a piece of intestine. This sample contained a dried bit of food—a little of the Iceman's last meal. Researchers studied the food with a scanning electron microscope (SEM), a microscope capable of magnifying a thousand times more than a regular microscope. They discovered undigested hop hornbeam pollen—pollen from trees that only bloom in the spring. So researchers concluded Oetzi must have died in the spring and not in the fall.

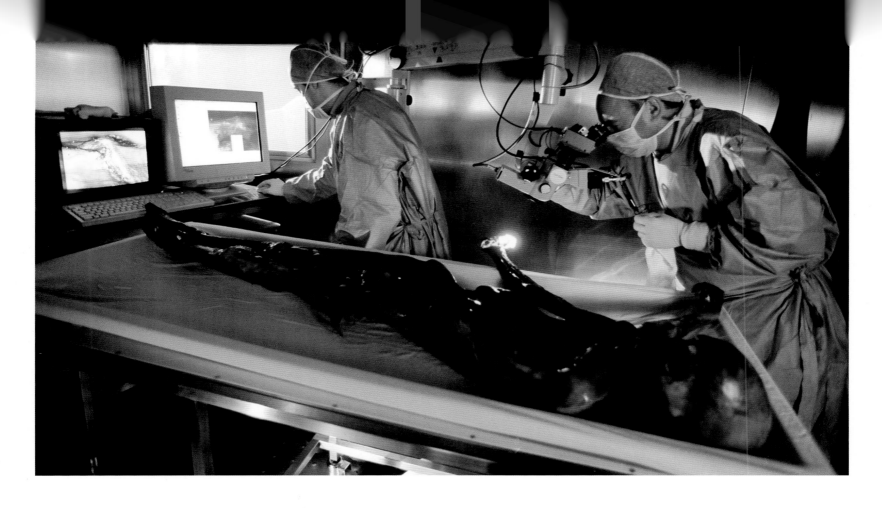

Here you can see researchers using another kind of camera connected to a computer to examine the Iceman's nearly closed hand. This revealed a wound no one had discovered before. It was a deep gash—the kind of wound police detectives see in someone who had to defend themselves from a knife attack. They concluded that the Iceman had probably fought with someone. Later, when researchers X-rayed Oetzi again, they discovered another new clue—an arrowhead lodged in the Iceman's shoulder. Its shape revealed it was the kind used in battles rather than for hunting. Researchers wondered if Oetzi died during a battle or if he was a murder victim after all.

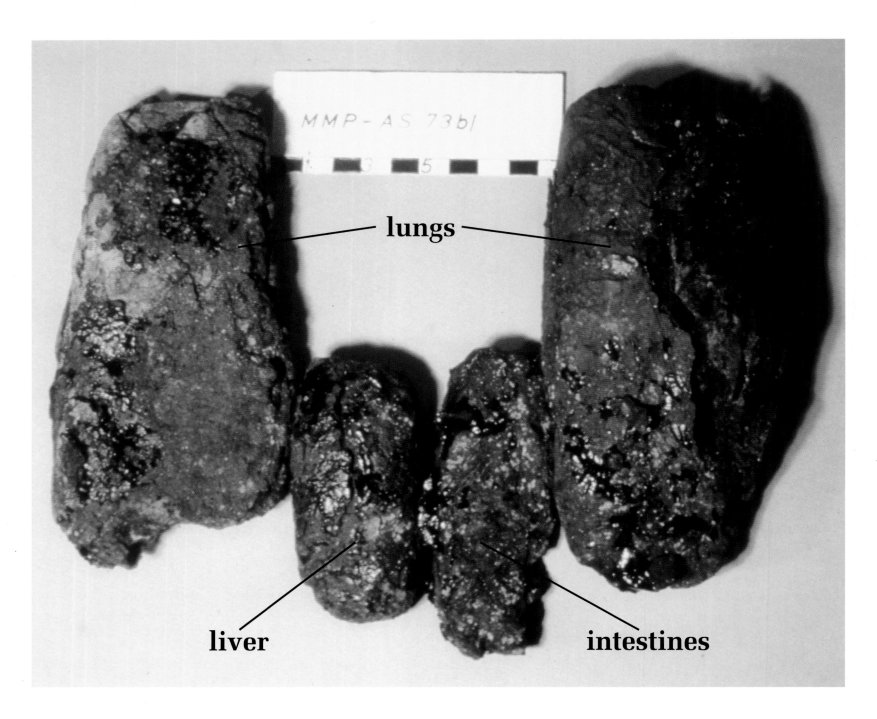

You may be surprised to learn what these are. They're mummified body organs.

In ancient Egypt, many people chose to have their loved ones mummified. There were three methods used to preserve the body. The cheapest left the organs inside the body during the mummification process. Because the soft parts easily rotted, this sometimes spoiled the body too. For a little more money, chemicals were injected into the body to dissolve the organs. Then the body was flushed out before being preserved. Those who could afford to pay even more had their loved one's organs carefully removed, dried, and placed in a container like this carved stone jar. Then the body was preserved and a kind of plant sap, called resin, was poured into the jar to preserve the organs too.

Researchers decided investigating a mummy's preserved lungs could reveal something about the person's health—could even provide clues about air quality at the time the mummified person was alive. First, they softened the tissue by soaking it in a liquid that mimicked the human body's natural fluid. Next, they sliced off pieces thinner than the thinnest paper and used this to make slides they could study with a microscope.

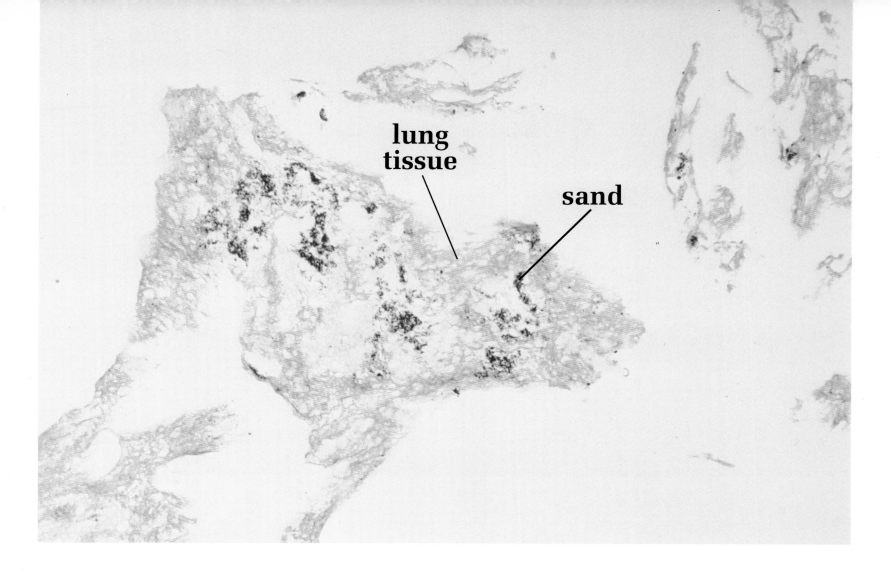

lung
tissue

sand

The researchers examined lung tissue from a number of different mummies. And, in as much as 80 percent of the samples, they discovered tiny black specks. So they removed some of these specks and conducted special chemical tests. They discovered the specks were silica—sand. Researchers also saw scarring in many of the lung tissue samples that they believed were caused from breathing in sand. These clues revealed that, like today, people living in ancient Egypt must have had to live through frequent sandstorms.

Here's something else researchers discovered ancient Egyptians had to live with. It's an adult schistosome worm, a kind of worm that lives inside people. This worm's larvae, or young, live in streams and rivers and bore through the skin of humans wading or swimming in the water. Once inside, the larvae develop into adult worms that mate and produce eggs. These lodge inside blood vessels, causing internal bleeding and other serious problems. This parasite is common in Egypt today. Researchers wondered how long ago people started being infected by this worm. And, they wondered whether a lot of or only a few people were infected in the past.

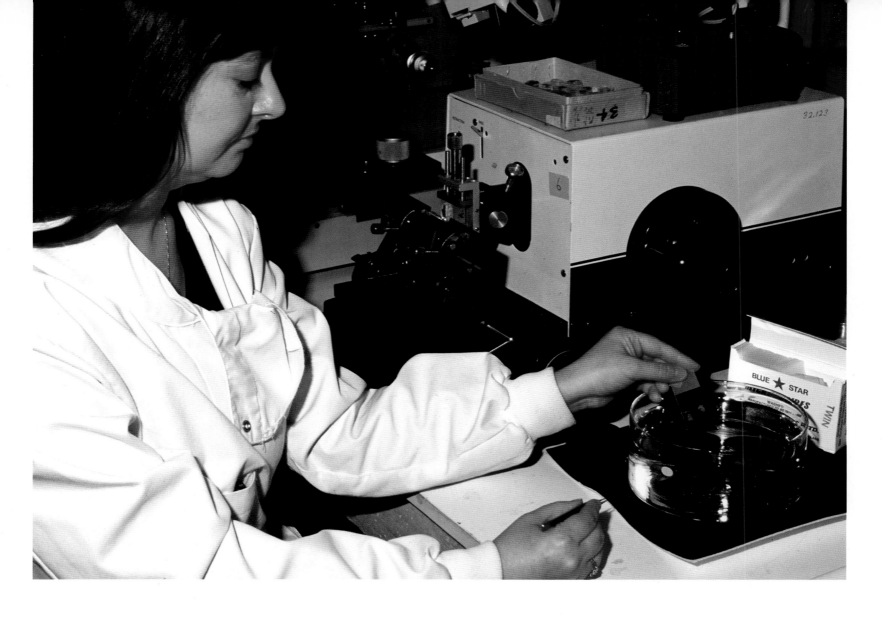

To solve these mysteries, researchers needed to look for schistosome worms and eggs in the tissue samples from many different ancient mummies. But first they had to figure out how to clean away thousands of years of dirt on mummified tissue. After a number of tests, they learned they could do that by rinsing the tissue with a strong acid. Then they were able to soften, slice, and prepare microscope slides.

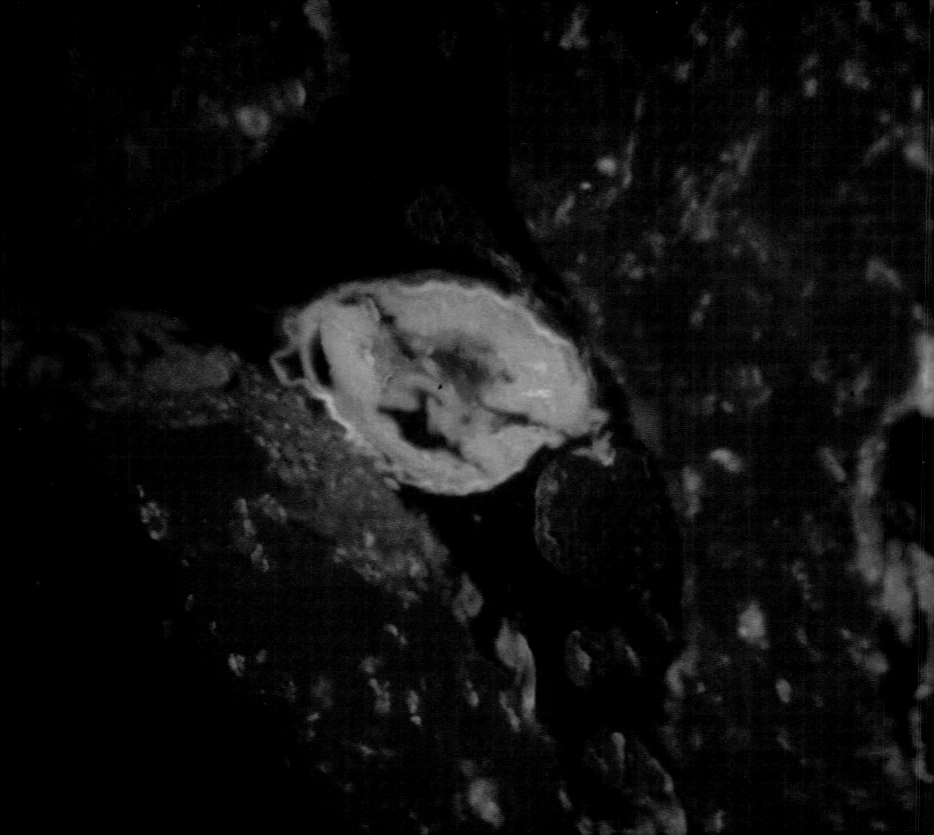

This bright green blob is a schistosome worm egg. Researchers discovered it when viewing tissue from a mummy believed to be about a thousand years old. To be able to easily spot the worm egg, the tissue was stained with a special fluorescent dye that would be picked up only by the worm's eggs and not by the human tissue. Then the slide was viewed through a special microscope that projected a fluorescent light, making any eggs that were present glow. About 25 percent of all of the ancient tissue samples tested this way contained schistosome eggs.

Researchers are still investigating to find the oldest mummy with schistosome infection. And they're still trying to determine how widespread schistosome infections were in the past. Nearly 300 million people are infected with schistosome worms today. So researchers hope that better understanding the history of this worm's spread through human populations might help them think of a way to stop its spread in the future.

In 1999, 22,000 feet (6,705 meters) up on the rugged slopes of Mount Llullaillaco (yoo-yeye-yah-ko), one of Argentina's highest volcanic mountains, researchers discovered an ancient Incan burial site. There, alongside gold statues and pots containing preserved food, they found the frozen, naturally mummified bodies of three children: a boy and two girls. One was the girl you saw on page 3.

How the children had died wasn't immediately clear, but researchers guessed because of the items found with them that these were human sacrifices. The ancient Incas had been known to sacrifice children as messengers to the gods, often on high mountain peaks to speed their travels. Researchers wondered where these children came from. The first step to solving that mystery was to study the mummies' DNA.

First, researchers collected a tiny tissue sample from each mummified child. They needed about a billion molecules to work with—a lot more than the tiny tissue sample could provide. But the researchers were able to use a special technique called PCR (polymerase chain reaction). This allows a little bit of DNA to be multiplied in much the same way a picture can be photocopied to get lots of exact duplicates. That gave the researchers enough material for a machine called a DNA sequencer to analyze.

And they made a surprising discovery—the two girls had probably been half sisters. Experts reading this set of DNA fingerprints discovered that the girls showed nine different common points. Because of the genes on which those points were located, researchers believed the girls may have had the same mother but different fathers. The boy's DNA, on the other hand, was different enough to suggest he had not been related to either of the girls.

Now, researchers plan to collect DNA samples from people living in communities at the base of Mount Llullaillaco. They're hoping this will let them find the living descendants of the mummified children's families. That may provide insights into what the mummified children were like. It would also help researchers better understand the history of the people living at the base of Mount Llullaillaco today.

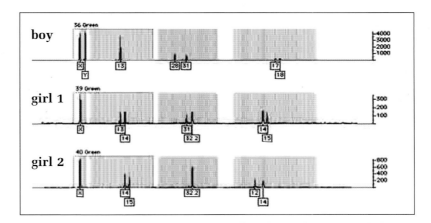

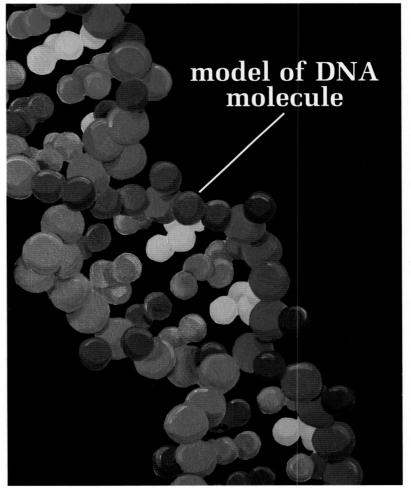

model of DNA molecule

When it comes to investigating mysteries about the ancient past, mummies are time capsules packed with clues. For example, new tests have revealed that there is even more to the story of Oetzi, the Iceman. When researchers analyzed the blood found on the Iceman's weapons, DNA tests revealed all of the blood was human, but none of it was Oetzi's. That makes researchers believe the Iceman probably fought with other people before he was killed— may even have seriously wounded one or more of them. But who did Oetzi fight with and when? And was one of those people the one that killed him? There are probably still more clues that new technologies will be able to reveal in the future.

Mummies are helping researchers learn about events that happened long ago. They are also revealing what it was like to be alive, be sick, and die in the ancient past. Who knows what clues mummies may yet reveal! One day, you could be the one to collect clues from mummies that let you solve mysteries about the past.

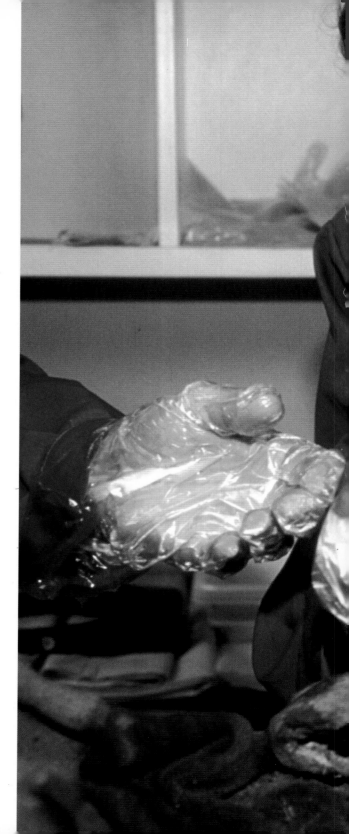

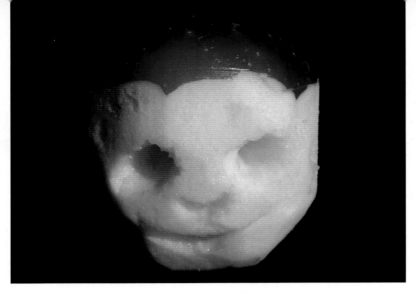

NATRON

In a mixing bowl, stir together 1 cup baking soda, 1 cup powdered all-fabric laundry bleach, and 1 cup table salt until well mixed. Prepare additional batches of natron as needed to cover the apple.

Make Your Own Mummy

See for yourself how the ancient Egyptians prepared mummies. Follow the recipe to whip up a simulated version of natron, a kind of salt that occurs naturally in some Egyptian desert areas and that was used in the mummification process. Then use it to produce a mummy—in this case, a mummified apple head.

First, have an adult peel an apple, leaving skin around the top as "hair." Use the sharpened end of a pencil and a spoon handle to give the apple eye sockets, a nose, ears, and a mouth. Next, pour a little natron into a mixing bowl. Or cut the top off a half-gallon (2-liter) plastic jug and use the bottom as your container. Set the apple on the natron and pour on more natron until the apple is almost completely covered. Don't worry about packing the natron into the eyes, ears, nose or mouth. Place the bowl in a warm, dry spot and leave it for a week. Mummifying a human, like the partly unwrapped body you can see on the book's cover, took about forty days to dry out the tissue enough to prevent any further decay.

Next, pour two tablespoons of white glue into a bowl and stir in two tablespoons of water. Cut 10-inch- (2.5-centimeter-) wide strips of paper towel. Drag one strip at a time across the glue solution and wrap around the mummified apple head. Press down the edges of the paper as you go. Continue until the head is completely covered. Add additional strips until the apple is no longer visible through the paper. Set the wrapped apple on a plate and let it dry overnight. Turn the apple over and let it continue to dry for a second day or until it feels completely dry to the touch. The Egyptians coated the linen wrappings with resin, the sticky sap from some plants, to seal out moisture.

While the apple is drying, select a cardboard box that is just a little bigger than the wrapped mummified apple head. Decorate this with a colorful face to represent the mummy inside. You may also want to add additional decorative pictures. The ancient Egyptians covered the mummy's case with hieroglyphics, picture writing that told about the person's life.

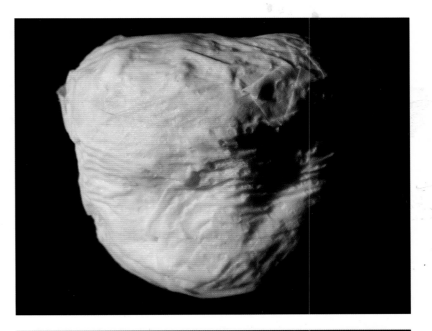

Glossary/Index

BONE   *bone*   One of the hard parts that forms the body's supporting frame or skeleton. **4, 5, 10, 11, 12**

BRAIN   *brayn*   Central body part that receives and analyzes messages about what is happening inside and outside the body. The brain sends instructions to put the body into action. **13**

CT SCAN   *kat skan*   An image produced through computer interpretation of X-ray images. **11, 12, 13, 19**

DNA   *dE-eN-A*   The abbreviation for the long chemical name (deoxyribonucleic acid) of the special part of every cell that stores all of the information needed for the cell to function. DNA also controls traits that are inherited or passed down from parent to child, such as hair color. **31–33**

ENDOSCOPE   *en-duh-skOp*   An instrument for seeing the inside of a hollow structure or body part. 20

ICEMAN   *Is-man*   The nickname given to the ancient mummy found in the Austrian Alps. **19–21**

LUNG   *luh-ng*   Body part where oxygen and carbon dioxide are exchanged. **10, 11, 22, 24, 25**

MICROSCOPE   *mI-kruh-skOp*   An instrument used to see a magnified view of whatever is being examined. **20, 24, 27, 29**

MUMMIFICATION   *muh-mi-fuh-KAY-shuhn*   The process, either artificial or natural, of preserving a body in order to prevent the tissue from decaying. **23, 36**

NATRON   *nA-truhn*   A special chemical used in ancient times as part of the mummification process. **36**

POLLEN   *PAH-lun*   The grains produced by flowers as part of their reproductive process. When combined with egg cells, seeds form. **19, 20**

RESIN   *re-zn*   Any of a number of solid and semi-solid substances produced by plants that was used as part of the mummification process in ancient times. **23, 37**

SCANNING ELECTRON MICROSCOPE (SEM)   *skan-ng E-lek-trawn mI-kruh-skOp*   A special kind of microscope able to magnify an image as much as a thousand times more than a regular microscope. **20**

SHCISTOSOME WORM *shis-tuh-sOm wuhrm*   A kind of worm that lives in and does damage to animals and humans. **26–29**

SKIN   *skin*   The external tissue covering the body. **3, 15, 26, 36**

SPIRAL COMPUTERIZED AXIAL TOMOGRAPHY SCANNER (See CT Scan)

TEETH   *tEth*   The hard bony structures in the jaws used for biting and grinding up food. **4**

X-RAY   *eks-rA*   An image produced by high-energy beams passing through something and striking a detection plate or special photographic film. **4, 16, 17**

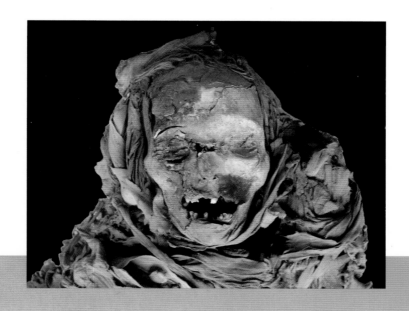

Wonder where the name *mummy* came from? It's from the Persian word *mummeia,* the name given to a tarry substance that just naturally oozed out of the ground. During the Middle Ages, between the fifth and fifteenth centuries, people used mummeia as medicine. They thought it would cure almost anything from headaches to diseases. Though natural mummeia wasn't easy to obtain, there were lots of ancient preserved human bodies. These looked like they were coated with mummeia because they were usually black from a coating of hardened resin. So creative businessmen started grinding up ancient bodies to sell as medicine. The name *mummeia*, which later became *mummy*, came to mean any preserved body.

With love for good friends Nancy Farrel and Mac McKeel

First published in the United States of America in 2005 by Walker Publishing Company, Inc.

Distributed to the trade by Holtzbrinck Publishers

For information about permission to reproduce selections from this book, write to Permissions, Walker & Company, 104 Fifth Avenue, New York, New York 10011

Book design by Victoria Allen

Visit Walker & Company's Web site at
www.walkeryoungreaders.com

Library of Congress Cataloging-in-Publication Data

Markle, Sandra.
Outside and inside mummies / Sandra Markle.
    p. cm.
Includes index.
ISBN 0-8027-8966-8 (HC) — ISBN 0-8027-8967-6 (RE)
 1. Mummies—Juvenile literature. 2. Mummies—Radiography—Juvenile literature. 3. Mummies—Pictorial works—Juvenile literature. I. Title.

GN293.M35 2005
393'.3—dc22

2004066128

ISBN-13 978-0-8027-8966-2
ISBN-13 978-0-8027-8967-9

Printed in Hong Kong
10 9 8 7 6 5 4 3 2 1

Acknowledgments: The author would like to thank the following people for sharing their enthusiasm and expertise. Dr. Larry W. Cartmell, Valley View Regional Hosptial, Oklahoma; Dr. John Connolly and Art Institute of Chicago, Rush University Medical Center, Illinois; Roger Fyfe and Canterbury Museum, Christchurch, New Zealand; Dr. Othmar Gaber, Institut fur Anatomie, Histologie und Embryologie der Universitat Innsbruck, Austria; Dr. Heidi Hoffman and Emory University Department of Radiology, Georgia; Michael Hurrell, Canterbury Health Board, Christchurch, New Zealand; Dr. Stephen Macko, University of Virginia–Charlottesville, Virginia; Dr. Keith McKenney, Clearant, Inc., Los California; Dr. James H. McKerrow, PhD, MD, University of California–San Francisco, California; Dr. Klaus Oeggl, Institut fur botanik der Leopold-Franzens-Universitat Innsbruk, Innsbruck, Austria; Brando Quilici, Brando Quilici Produzioni, Rome, Italy; Dr. Johan Reinhard, National Geographic Society explorer-in-residence, senior fellow at the Mountain Institute, West Virginia, and research associate of Chicago's Field Museum of Natural History; Dr. Patricia Rutherford, Centre for Biomedical Egyptology at the University of Manchester, Manchester, UK; Dr. Daniel Sawyer, DDS., PhD, Professor and Chair Department of Oral Diagnosis and Radiology, Assisant Dean for Diactic Education, Case School of Dental Medicine, Ohio; Neil Staff, Diagnostic Radiographer, Xograph Imaging Systems, Gloucestershire, UK, and Dr. Malcolm Jones, Molecular Parasitology Unit, Queensland Institute of Medical Research, Australia.

Also for their special contributions of mummies and tissue samples to the experts cited, the author would like to thank the Manchester Museum at the University of Manchester, the Munich Museum of Anthropology, the British Museum, Professor Doenhoff at the University of Bangor, Wales, and Roxie Walker. Finally, a special thank you to Skip Jeffery for his efforts and his loving support through the creative process.

Note to Parents and Teachers: The books in the Outside and Inside series enable young readers to discover how scientists, often working as a team, use different methods or procedures to investigate and sometimes develop new technologies or procedures to enable them to learn even more.

Photo Credits

Cover: courtesy of Dr. Heidi Hoffman and Emory University Department of Radiology
Page 1:   courtesy of Brando Quillici
Page 2:   courtesy of Johan Reinhard
Page 4:   courtesy of Art Institute of Chicago, Rush University Medical Center and Dr. John Connolly
Page 5:   courtesy of Dr. Heidi Hoffman and Emory University Department of Radiology
Page 6:   courtesy of Neil Staff, Xograph Imaging Systems
Page 7:   courtesy of Neil Staff, Xograph Imaging Systems
Page 8:   courtesy of Neil Staff, Xograph Imaging Systems
Page 10:   courtesy of Dr. Heidi Hoffman and Emory University Department of Radiology

Page 12:   courtesy of Canterbury Museum
Page 13:   courtesy of Art Institute of Chicago, Rush University Medical Center and Dr. John Connolly
Page 14:   courtesy of Art Institute of Chicago, Rush University Medical Center and Dr. John Connolly
Page 16:   courtesy of Johan Reinhard
Page 17:   courtesy of Danny Sawyer
Page 18:   courtesy of Brando Quillici
Page 20:   courtesy of Dr. Othmar Gaber; courtesy of Dr. Klaus Oeggl
Page 21:   courtesy of Brando Quillici
Page 22:   courtesy of Dr. James H. McKerrow
Page 23:   courtesy of Skip Jeffery

Page 24:   courtesy of Danny Sawyer
Page 25:   courtesy of Dr. James H. McKerrow
Page 26:   courtesy of Malcolm Jones
Page 27:   courtesy of Dr. Patricia Rutherford, KNH Center for Biomedical Egyptology, The University of Manchester, Oxford Road, Manchester, M139PT
Page 28:   courtesy of Dr. Patricia Rutherford
Page 30:   courtesy of Johan Reinhard
Page 32:   courtesy of Johan Reinhard
Page 33:   courtesy of Dr. Keith McKenney
Page 35:   courtesy of Johan Reinhard
Page 36:   courtesy of Skip Jeffery
Page 37:   courtesy of Skip Jeffery